The SCIENCE BEHIND the ATHLETE

India James

FOOTBALL

A Crabtree Crown Book

Crabtree Publishing
crabtreebooks.com

School-to-Home Support for Caregivers and Teachers

This appealing book is designed to teach students about core subject areas. Students will build upon what they already know about the subject, and engage in topics that they want to learn more about. Here are a few guiding questions to help readers build their comprehensions skills. Possible answers appear here in red.

Before Reading:

What do I know about football?

- *I know football is a sport.*
- *I know football players wear safety gear.*

What do I want to learn about this topic?

- *I want to know what kind of gear the first football players wore.*
- *I want to learn how science is helping keep players safe.*

During Reading:

I'm curious to know...

- *I'm curious to know how cleats are made.*
- *I'm curious to know how shoulder pads have changed.*

How is this like something I already know?

- *I know players wear different kinds of cleats.*
- *I know players wear different gear today than they did in the past.*

After Reading:

What was the author trying to teach me?

- *The author was trying to teach me what helmets are made of.*
- *The author was trying to teach me how technology has changed in football.*

How did the photographs and captions help me understand more?

- *The photographs helped me understand how science has improved the game of football.*
- *The captions gave me extra information about the history of football.*

TABLE OF CONTENTS

WHAT IS FOOTBALL?

American football has been around since the 1800s. The first college football game was played in 1869. It was more like **rugby** than the football game we know now.

FOOTBALL FACT

Many people in the world use the word "football" to refer to the sport that Americans call "soccer." American football is played with eleven-person teams on a rectangular field that is 100 yards long.

Rule changes in the 1880s made the game more like the game of football that is played today. These changes also made football more dangerous. Science has since helped make the game safer.

FOOTBALL FACT

Early football was so dangerous that 19 people are said to have died playing the game in 1905.

1

HELMETS

Tackling has been part of football since it was first played. When players fall to the ground, they can injure their heads. Helmets help protect players.

Leather football helmet believed to have been worn by Gerald Ford, president of the United States from 1974-1977, while playing for the University of Michigan, 1932-1934

Reeves in 1929

FOOTBALL FACT

Joseph Mason Reeves was one of the first people to wear a helmet while playing football. In 1893, he asked a shoemaker to make a moleskin hat with ear flaps, which he wore to his next game.

HELMET HISTORY

For the first 50 years of the game, most players did not wear helmets. The players who did, put thin pieces of leather with a bit of padding on their heads.

A football team in 1910

The first plastic helmet was created in 1939. Soon, foam and padding were added. Leather was also used as a protective layer. Some helmets even contained inflatable air cushions. Facemasks, a part of the helmet that protects a player's face, were first added in the 1950s.

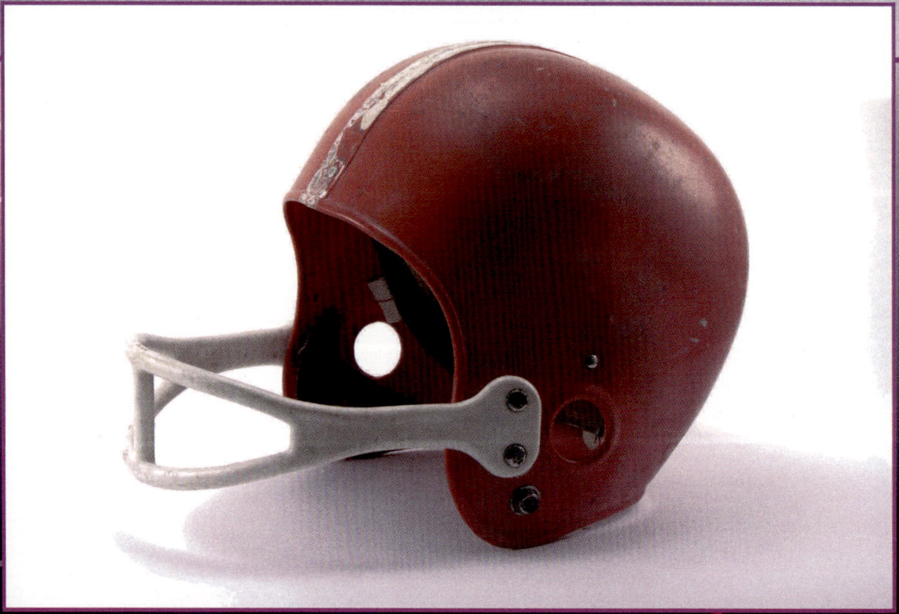

HELMET TECHNOLOGY

Helmet radios help coaches talk with players during a game. Coaches can call plays while on the sidelines. Radios have often caused problems. Sometimes they cut out when important information is needed. Making reliable helmet radios is important for football players and coaches.

HEAD INJURIES

Head injuries are one of the biggest concerns in football today. Hits taken by players have been linked to a condition called **Traumatic Brain Injury** (TBI). Serious TBI can lead to brain damage. This brain damage can lead to **depression** and contribute to early death.

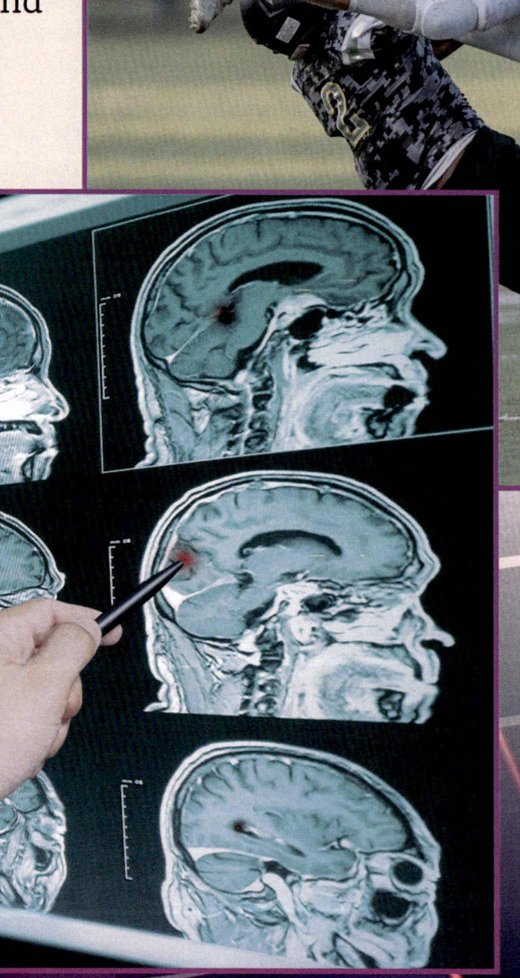

Scientists are working to make helmets better to prevent head injuries. They run tests with sensors to help understand the forces that result in head injuries. This can help them design helmets to withstand these kinds of hits.

2 SHOULDER PADS

SHOULDER PAD HISTORY

Shoulder pads help protect a football player's upper body. The first football players didn't use shoulder pads. Like other aspects of safety, shoulder pads developed with the game. Shoulder pads first appeared in the late 1800s.

Early shoulder pads in 1906

The first shoulder pads were made of several layers of cloth. Then players began wearing shoulder pads that were made of leather and wool. Today, shoulder pads are made of a hard plastic outer layer with foam underneath.

CANTILEVERED SHOULDER PADS

All shoulder pads are now made with plastic and foam, but that doesn't mean all shoulder pads are alike!

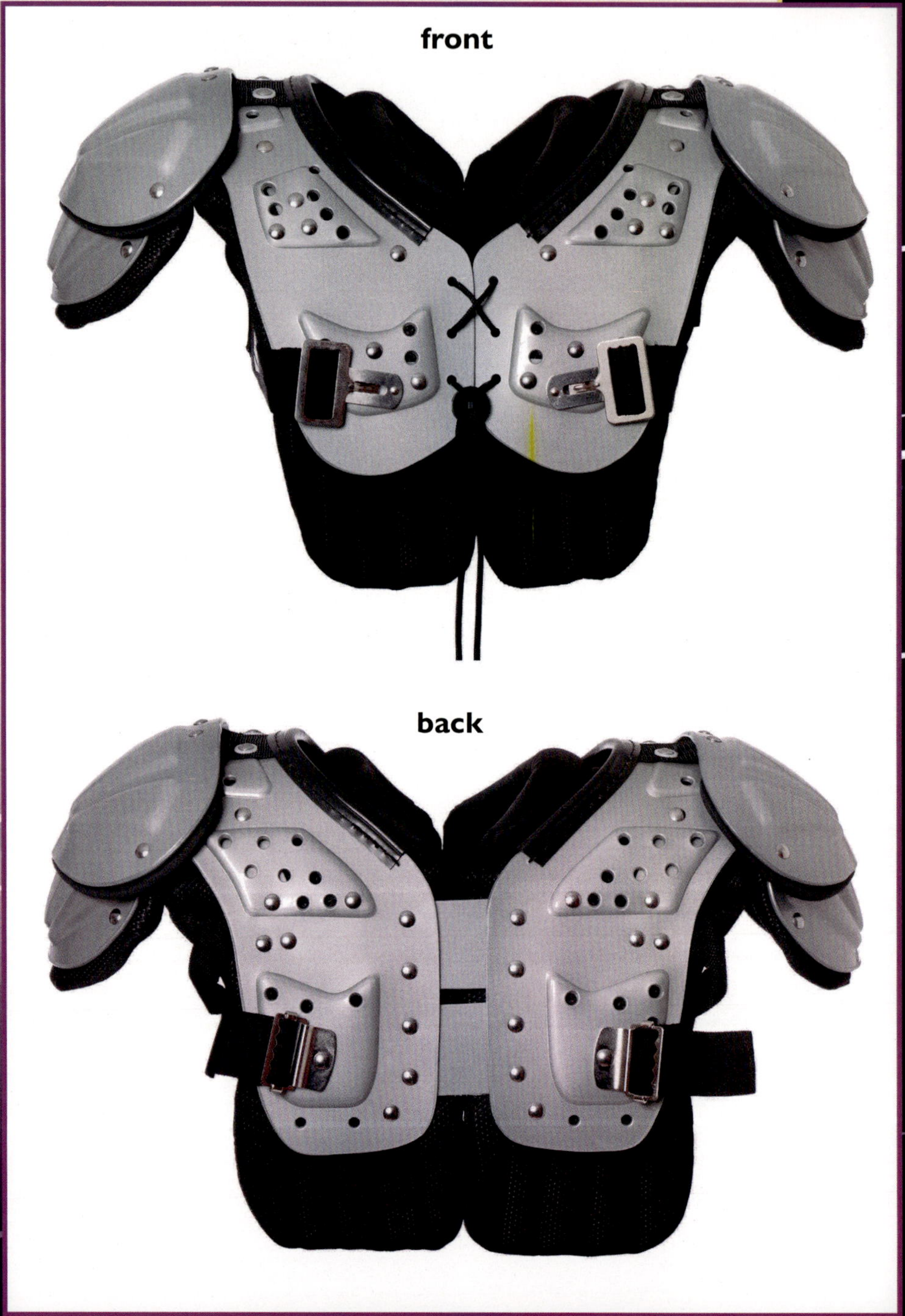

front

back

Cantilevered pads spread out the force from a hit and send it into the pad's cushion, instead of a player's shoulder. This type of shoulder pad is bigger and bulkier than noncantilevered pads. Players in positions that block and tackle use cantilevered pads. Younger players and players in positions that do not block and tackle often use noncantilevered shoulder pads, which are lighter and allow for more movement.

CHANGING SHOULDER PADS

Shoulder pads today have become smaller and lighter. Many players prefer smaller shoulder pads because they feel they improve their speed and movement, but player safety is still more important. Team doctors and coaches keep an eye on how often players are injured. If players are not injured any more often with a smaller pad, then players are allowed to continue with this newer design.

FOOTBALL FACT

Today, shoulder pads in the National Football League (NFL) weigh less than 4 pounds (1.8 kg). In the early 2000s, they could weigh as much as 8 pounds (3.6 kg).

Changes in playing surfaces also mean that smaller shoulder pads can be used. From the 1970s to the 1990s, many teams often played on artificial turf. This surface was usually hard and led to injuries. Softer surfaces began to be used instead. Because players today fall on softer surfaces, they can use smaller pads without getting injured. Changes in rules about tackling have also helped keep players safe.

3

CLEATS

CLEAT HISTORY

Football players have been using cleats since the first days of the game. Cleats are shoes with **studs** in the sole that help a player's foot grip a soft or slippery field. The first cleats were made using wood, leather, and metal.

FOOTBALL FACT

It's believed that the first pair of cleats was created in the 1500s for King Henry VIII of England. It's not known though if he actually used them for sports!

After the invention of **vulcanized rubber**, cleats became lighter in the 1920s. Today, cleats are highly specialized to each position and type of player.

Most tires are made of vulcanized rubber.

FOOTBALL FACT

In 1925, removable studs were developed. Players walked home in the same shoes they played in after taking off the studs!

CLEAT TECHNOLOGY

The amount, location, and shape of stud differs by the position being played. Receivers want cleats that help them run fast. Running backs and linemen need cleats that help them change direction quickly.

Players can use computer programs to test different arrangements of cleats. These programs let them see how the shoe reacts to different surfaces and forces.

Even the material of the studs themselves have improved since cleats were first used. Engineers have developed a coating that repels mud and water. This "anti-clog" technology prevents mud from building up on the bottom of the cleats.

quarterback

wide receiver

linebacker

running back

4 TRAINING AND PLAYING THE GAME

Equipment isn't the only aspect of football that has changed because of technology. The way players train and play the game have also evolved because of science.

RULES FOR SAFETY

Since 2002, the NFL has made more than 50 rule changes to help keep players safe. During the game, **instant replay** allows referees and officials to determine if players are acting in an unsafe manner.

DURING THE GAME

The technology football coaches use has also improved. For a long time, coaches were given black-and-white printed pictures of how the team played. Recently, the NFL has begun providing tablets to coaches during the game for immediate, color pictures of their players. This helps by giving the coaches faster feedback with a better picture.

TECHNOLOGY TROUBLE

Technology doesn't always advance smoothly. When instant replay was introduced in the NFL in 1986, it didn't work fast enough to be useful. After six years of use, instant replay was stopped until technology improved in 1999.

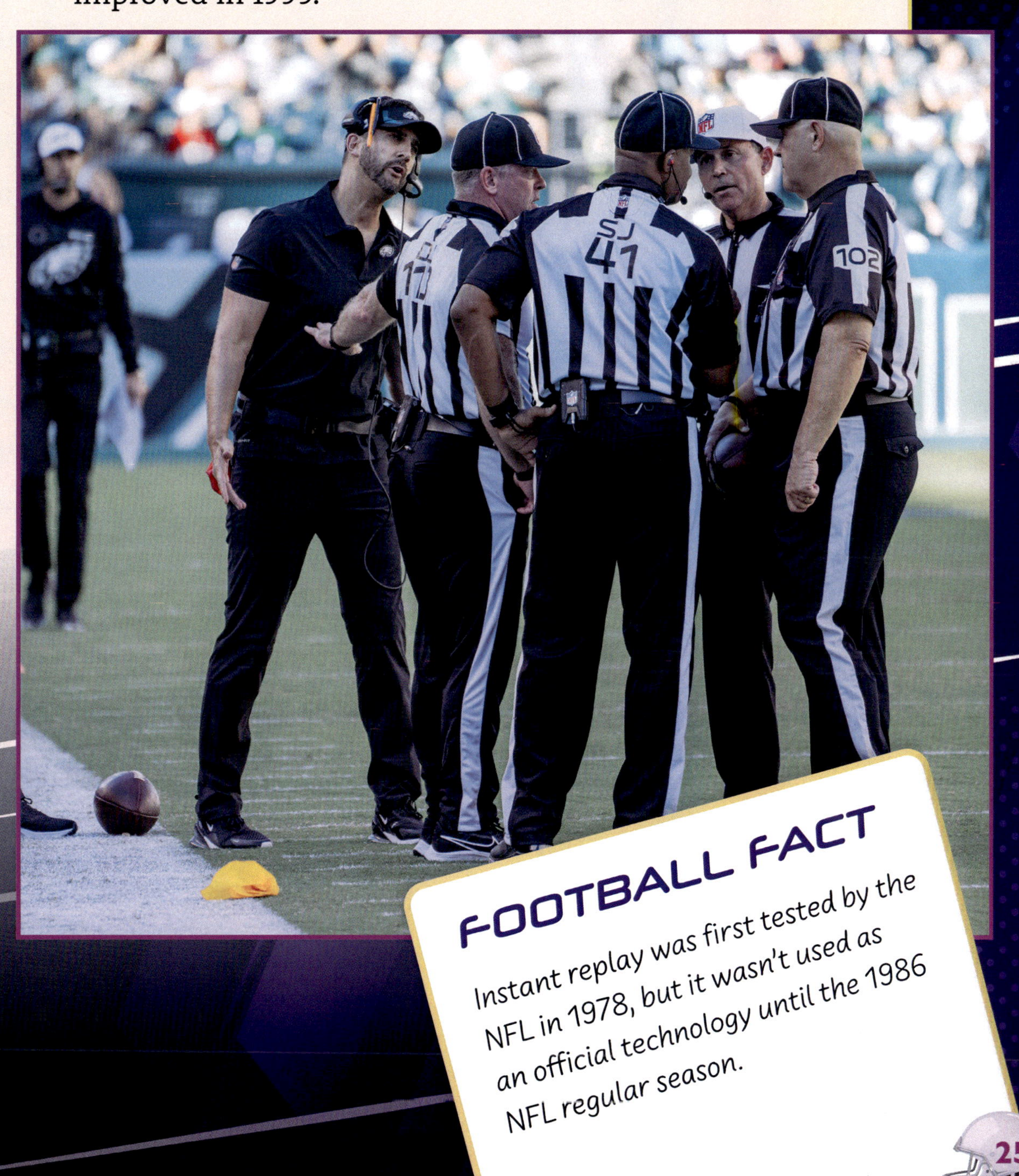

FOOTBALL FACT

Instant replay was first tested by the NFL in 1978, but it wasn't used as an official technology until the 1986 NFL regular season.

5 STATISTICS

Touchdowns and tackles might be the most exciting parts of the game, but football is a sport that depends a lot on math. **Statistics** is one area where math is used to help understand the game.

STATISTICS

Statistics is an area of math that collects, organizes, and **analyzes** sets of numbers. In football, statistics are used to explain how players are performing and how the team is doing overall. Coaches, scouts, and the media all use statistics to understand how players and teams are performing.

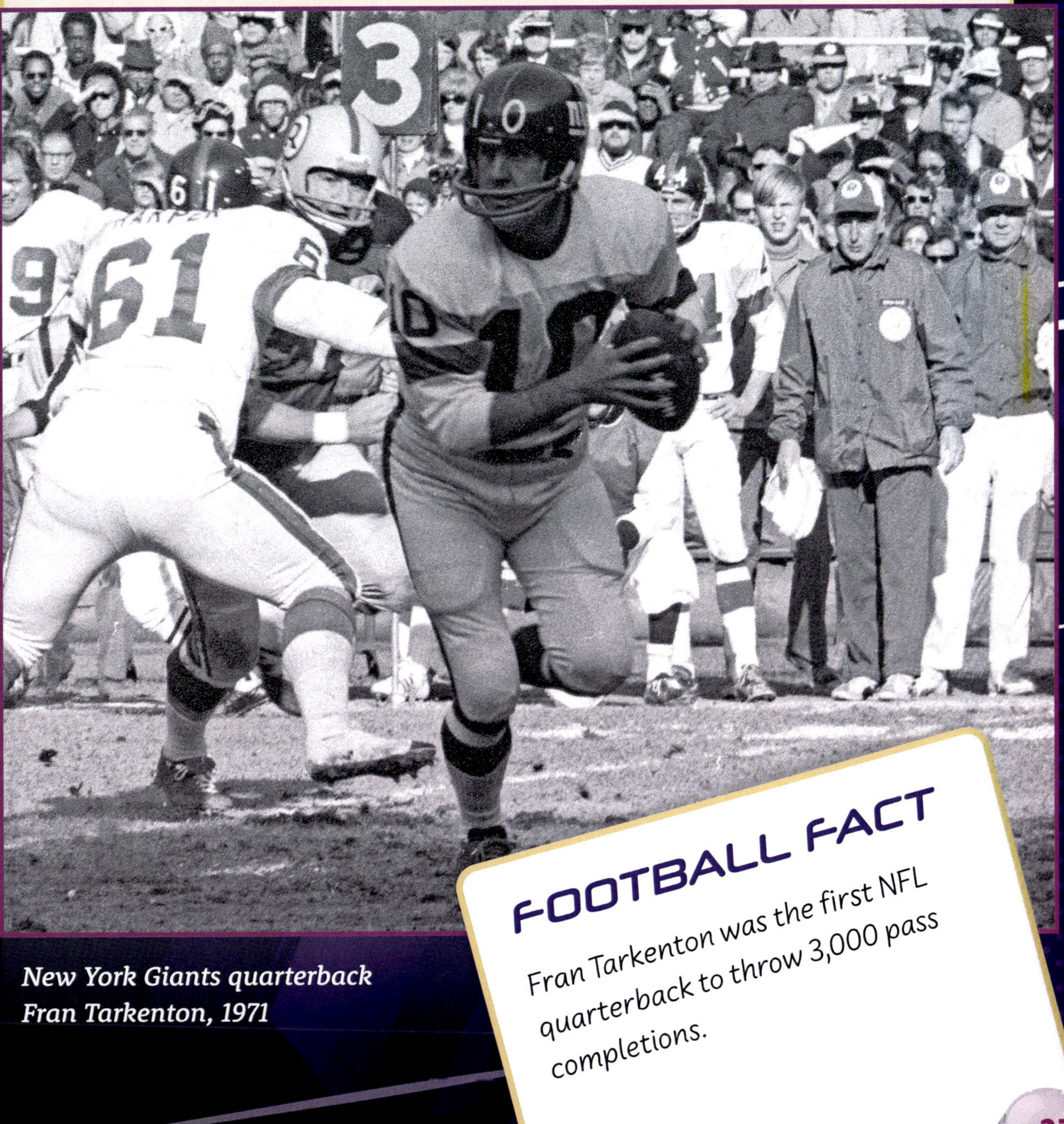

New York Giants quarterback Fran Tarkenton, 1971

FOOTBALL FACT

Fran Tarkenton was the first NFL quarterback to throw 3,000 pass completions.

PROJECTION STATISTICS

Sometimes statistics are used to try and predict how well a team will do in the future. Scouts also use this information to help decide which players to recruit for their team.

The more information a person has, the better their statistics will be. Football has a short season. Sometimes it is hard to get enough information to calculate meaningful statistics.

NFL and other professional league scouts take down time results during a college football pro day. A pro day is an event where college football players show their skills.

CONCLUSION

Football players are athletes that play a dangerous and exciting game. The helmets, pads, rules, and training have changed since the first time football was played. Science and technology can help make the sport more exciting and safer in the future.

GLOSSARY

analyze (AN-uh-lize): To examine carefully and in detail

cantilevered pads (KAN-tl-ee-ver-ed pads): Bulky shoulder pads that cushion a force by directing it into the pad instead of the shoulder

depression (dih-PRESH-uhn): A serious mood disorder that causes extreme sadness that lasts more than a few days

instant replay (IN-stuhnt REE-pley): A video recording of an action that can be played back, often in slow motion

rugby (RUHG-bee): A full-contact team sport where players try to carry or kick a ball over the opposing team's goal line

statistics (stuh-TIS-tiks): A branch of math that collects, organizes, and analyzes numbers

studs (stuhdz): Individual extensions on the bottom of a shoe that grip into the ground

tackle (TAK-uhl): To force the player with the ball to fall to the ground

traumatic brain injury (truh-MAT-ik breyn IN-juh-ree): The result of a hard hit to the head that affects how the brain works

vulcanized rubber (VUHL-kun-nahyzd RUHB-er): A type of rubber that has been hardened to make it last longer

INDEX

COMPREHENSION QUESTIONS

1. When was the first college football game played?
   a. 1990
   b. 1869
   c. 1735
2. Which material was used in the first helmets?
   a. leather
   b. sheep stomach
   c. rubber
3. What material was used to make football cleats lighter?
   a. nylon
   b. wool
   c. vulcanized rubber
4. **True or False:** Math is important in football.
5. **True or False:** Helmets have been used since the start of football.

Answers: 1. B, 2. A, 3. C, 4. True, 5. False

ABOUT THE AUTHOR

India James writes about science, technology, and math for young readers. She loves when science comes together with sports. India lives in Ohio with her family.

Written by: India James
Designed by: Kathy Walsh
Series Development: James Earley
Proofreader: Melissa Boyce
Educational Consultant: Marie Lemke M.Ed.

Photographs: Shutterstock; Cover & Title pg: Mike Orlov, Lilo Alfonso, geen graphy, your; p 2-31 backgrounds: Lilo Alfonso, your; pg numbers: AK_Vector; p 4: Marco Iacobucci Epp, Daniel Padavona; p 5: Library of Congress; p 6: @Wiki; p 7: @Wiki, Brocreative; p 8: Jeffrey M Horler, Everett Collection; p 9 Richard Paul Kane, Ken Murray/Icon Sportswire; p 10: Margaret Kite, April stock; p 11: DC Studio, Rocketclips, Inc.; p 12: @Wiki, Everett Collection; p 13: Paul Orr, LumenVision; p 14: Dan Thornberg; p 15: Juan Lainex/Marinmedia/Csm; p 16: Fred Kfoury III/Icon Sportswire; p 17: Mark Goldman/Icon Sportswire; p 18: Lorna Roberts, Gemenacom; p 19: nikkytok; p 20: Scott Serio; p 21: Rich Graessle/Icon Sportswire, Mark Alberti/Icon Sportsire, Bailey Hillesheim/Icon Sportswire; p 22: Stan Szeto; p 23: Andy Lewis/Icon Sportswire; p 24: Dough Murray/Icon Sportswire; p 25: Jim Z. Rider; p 26: John Sommers II; p 27: Arnie Sachs; p 28: Andrew Fielding; p 29: Beto Chagas

Crabtree Publishing

crabtreebooks.com 800-387-7650

Printed in Canada/012024/CP20231127

Published in Canada
Crabtree Publishing
616 Welland Ave.
St. Catharines, Ontario
L2M 5V6

Published in the United States
Crabtree Publishing
347 Fifth Ave
Suite 1402-145
New York, NY 10016

Library and Archives Canada Cataloguing in Publication
Available at Library and Archives Canada

Library of Congress Cataloging-in-Publication Data
Available at the Library of Congress

Hardcover: 978-1-0398-3894-9
Paperback: 978-1-0398-3979-3
Ebook (pdf): 978-1-0398-4053-9
Epub: 978-1-0398-4125-3